HARRY CHAMBERS & PETERLOO POETS

37 Years of Poetry Publishing

Harry Chambers (1976) photo: Malcolm Mort

HARRY CHAMBERS & PETERLOO POETS

37 Years of Poetry Publishing

John Lucas

*For Eric Panton
from the young man
on the left.*

*Harry Chambers
10th March 2009*

First published in 2009 by Peterloo Poets
The Old Chapel, Sand Lane, Calstock, Cornwall PL18 9QX, U.K.

© John Lucas, 2009

The moral rights of the author are asserted in accordance with the
Copyright, Designs and Patent Act, 1988

All rights reserved. No part of this publication may be reproduced,
stored in a retrieval system, or transmitted, in any form or by any
means, electronic, mechanical, photocopying, recording or otherwise
without the prior permission in writing of the publisher.

A catalogue record for this book is available
from the British Library

ISBN 978-1-90-432451-5

Poetry and small presses seem to belong naturally together. You have only to look at any quarter's publications listed by the Poetry Book Society to see that this is so. Alongside books from Cape, Faber, Picador, and, very occasionally, Chatto, you will invariably find work under the imprint of well-funded and securely established independent presses: Anvil, Bloodaxe, Carcanet, Enitharmon, Seren. But by far the largest number of books and smaller collections comes from a host of presses that are by and large one-person organizations: Arc, Five Leaves, Flambard, Happenstance, Mariscat, Perdika, Redbeck, Shearsman, my own Shoestring, Worple, for example. Because the survival of any of these depends on imponderables – in particular the uncertain continuation of funds, enthusiasm and good health – they tend to come and go at fairly regular intervals. Only one seems to go on for ever. Harry Chambers began Peterloo Poets in the mid 1970s. In those far-off days the weeklies and broadsheets took seriously their responsibility to review new poetry, and they were quite prepared to give a welcome to new publishers. The only proviso was that the work had to be of reasonable quality. With the exception of one reviewer in the *Sunday Times*, who greeted each book as though it was a work of five-star genius, collections from the smallest and most evanescent of presses were treated with the same seriousness as publications from the long-established houses. It therefore says a great deal about Peterloo that from the outset its books were both widely and favourably noticed. And what it chiefly says is that in the matter of choosing who to publish and how to produce their books, its publisher was clearly blessed with the shrewd good taste without which no small press can hope to survive for long. As a result, Peterloo Poets was by the end of the decade more or less taken for granted as a component of the scene. It has remained one ever since.

But chance didn't crown Harry king of the small presses without his stir. "We try to choose a life" the American poet W.D.Snodgrass wrote, in a poem addressed to his daughter. His remark isn't one I'd expect to find issuing from Harry Chambers' lips. Or rather, the tone of Snodgrass's words – in which attempted exculpation is tinged with a rueful acceptance of the many roads not taken – doesn't strike me as at all Chambersonian. If anyone was born to be a small-press publisher, it's Harry Chambers, and no *hélas* about it. He has all the necessary ingredients: flair, determination, the bonhomie that befits a man who loves good food and drink and conversation, coupled with a certain steeliness of resolve, and, most important of all, a sure sense of the poetry of which he most approves and wants to promote.

This spreads surprisingly wide, at all events if you think, as some do, that Peterloo exists to further the cause of what they disparagingly call "mainstream" poetry, by which they mean a poetry that is incuriously complacent, formal in traditional ways, in a word, tame. Such poetry is, of course, not mainstream at all, but – to continue the riverine metaphor – backwater. My guess is that "mainstream" entered the language of art and aesthetics in the 20th century as a way of defining the kind of jazz that, according to the O.E.D., is "neither traditional nor modern." It's therefore applied to the work of, among others, Teddy Wilson, Billie Holiday, Coleman Hawkins, Buck Clayton, and Lester Young, each of whom would surely be accepted as unequivocally great musicians. Yet in poetry "mainstream" is a term most often used by those for whom it does mean "backwater". No need to ask which names in particular belong among this pensioned-off fleet of rusting hulks: Larkin and Heaney.

Harry Chambers's lifelong devotion to Philip Larkin is a matter of public record. When I was preparing this piece, I asked him if he had ever hoped or wanted to be a poet. Poetry is, after all, the literary art form that he dearly loves and which he's served for over forty years. Yes, he said, ruefully. He'd written poems at and after university, but having read *The Less Deceived* in his second year at Liverpool he realised that Larkin was writing the type of poem he himself had hoped to write, but doing it far better than he could ever dream of doing. Still, he did go on to write a parody of Hamlet's "Hecuba" speech – the one where he instructs the players how best to act their parts – in the voice of Larkin, and this won him £10.00 in a *New Statesman* competition. It runs:

I am a tired old fart but, shit a brick,
It makes me puke to see a guy on stage,
Some jeans-and-sneakers Protest-Theater prick,
Eyes blorting tears, pull all the stops. My age
He'd have some cause to moan his fouled-up luck:
What's *Monica* to him? He wouldn't give a fuck.

Their tastes in jazz are similar, too. I recall one bibulous afternoon at Calstock in 1988 when Harry wanted me to hear an old Muggsy Spanier 78 rpm which he proposed to play on a wind-up gramophone he had managed to disinter from somewhere in the house. With elaborate care he freed the shellac record from its card cover, wiped it, positioned it on the turntable, then began to wind the machine – alas with too great vigour. From deep inside the box came a rending sound as of wood parting company from screws, followed by a clang. We heard no more that day.

This was a few years after Harry had edited for Peterloo *An Enormous Yes: in memoriam Philip Larkin (1922-1985)*, published exactly a year after Larkin's death. Rather more than ten years earlier, proof of an enduring love, a special double issue of the magazine *Phoenix* (11/12 – 1973/4) of which Harry was founder-editor had been given over to Larkin and this invaluable publication, which contains Larkin worksheets for "At Grass", the first appearance of "Money", and several poems and critical articles, is now a collector's item. Later in the 1980s, Blackwell Rare Books were asking £30 for *Phoenix 11/12*, and last year Harry received a catalogue from P & B Rowan, Antiquarian and Fine Books, Belfast, in which the asking price for a set of *Phoenix, 1-13*, was £750.

I imagine that the entire run of the magazine in its two manifestations would fetch an even higher price. The first version began as a student literary journal, in the days when every university and college had literary magazines, many of them now highly valued *trouvées*. Harry launched himself on an editorial career as a Liverpool University undergraduate, where, having survived national service, he went in 1958 to study English. Among the student contributors to the *Phoenix* was Landeg White; and Kenneth Allott, although his own days as poet were long behind him, kept a watching brief. I've no idea what kind of a stir the journal made, but at least those who were unaware of its editor's presence had it drawn to their attention when he organised an exhibition by the anarchically-minded Liverpool sculptor, Arthur Dooley. Most of the pieces in the show were priced at between £10 and £25, but there was one notable exception. The huge centrepiece of the exhibition, labelled "Mother and Child, Liverpool, 1960", and priced at £1,000, consisted of a drainpipe nailed to a vertical, jagged-ended railway sleeper. At a key moment during the opening of the exhibition, a masked figure wielding an axe and closely followed by a local press photographer – Dooley always had an eye for publicity – burst in and hacked the sculpture down. When interviewed after-wards, Dooley explained that this was his protest against Liverpool City's housing policy. It did him no harm. He was commissioned to provide a metal mural for Liverpool's Catholic Cathedral, then under construction. Typically, he provided a soldier in his Stations of the Cross with a CND badge.

Having completed his undergraduate career with some distinction, Harry spent a year training to be a teacher. Then began a schoolmasterly career, first at the Grammar school in South Yorkshire where he himself had been a pupil. He quit this post over a matter of principle and without having a job to go to. But almost at once he landed work as a lecturer in a teacher training college, in Belfast, where his hero, Larkin, had put in some years as a university librarian. It was here, I think, that his life as editor-publisher really began. He attended some of the famous meetings that Philip Hobsbaum ran, at which poets would gather to discuss work handed in by a member of the group. (The poet whose verses were being discussed was required to remain silent throughout.) Hobsbaum had begun this practice in London, where he brought together a number of young poets who called themselves "The Group" – they included George Macbeth and the Peters Porter and Redgrove – though it is wrong to claim, as he and others have since done, that he was the first to create such a critical in-house grouping. In an admittedly less formal way, G.S.Fraser had in the immediate post-war years used his living quarters in Chelsea to play host to poets for readings and discussion of work-in-progress, and soon after I got to Reading in 1956 I found that John Wain, although no longer a lecturer at the University there, would from time to time summon a number of aspiring writers to his flat in order to meet practising poets who were passing through. Richard Murphy, Christopher Middleton and, one drink-soaked evening, Theodore Roethke, were among those to be encountered at Wain's flat on Brunswick Street. The meetings invariably became the occasion for hard-knuckled discussion of work that one or another writer had brought along. As a non-writer, Harry didn't last at the Hobsbaum gatherings. But before being banished he met the young Seamus Heaney and Michael Longley, both of whom would feature in the revived *Phoenix*, as would Derek Mahon, who, like Harry, never fell under the Hobsbaum spell.

By the end of the 1960s Harry was back in England, this time as a lecturer in English at Didsbury College of Education, where he was to meet his future wife, Lynn. Now, a new venture began. Phoenix pamphlets began as an off-shoot of the magazine. The first series of these pamphlets, "Edited by Harry Chambers & Eric J.Morten" appeared early in 1969. The six poets chosen were Glyn Hughes, *Love on the Moor*, Michael Longley, *Secret Marriages*, Seamus Heaney, *A Lough Neagh Sequence*, (it would be incorporated into his as-yet unpublished second collection, *Door Into the Dark*), John Ashbrook, *Death Duties*, Harold Massingham, *The Magician*, and Jim Burns, *The Store of Things*. Heaney and Longley apart, the poets were all young men who at that time lived and worked in the North West, and, Massingham excepted, were relatively unknown. (*Love on the Moor* would rightly bring Glyn Hughes much praise and inevitably attracted the attention of other publishers. His next, prize-winning book was published by Macmillan, after which he turned for a while to fiction and won the *Guardian* Fiction prize.) The pamphlets, saddle-stitched and with white gloss-laminated covers, all bore variants on the *Phoenix* colophon, with the exception of Heaney's, which has on the cover a design that looks to have a seine net held by a Celtic ring. Each pamphlet carried the information that, if you were prepared to pay more than the 3/- (15p new money) which was the asking price for each pamphlet, "The first 50 copies of this limited edition of 1,000 are signed by the author, numbered, bound in hard covers and priced at £1.1.0".

A *limited edition of 1,000.* Anyone reading this in 2009 can only blink in amazement at such figures. They will also, surely, be mightily impressed by the judgement of an editor who could begin with such a winners' list of authors. I imagine, though, that the 1,000 print run came to seem over-ambitious. And so, when the second series came out the following year, now priced at 20p, the print-run was lower. Not that the quality of work was in any way lessened. This group of six included pamphlets by John Mole, Christopher Pilling, George Kendrick, Stanley Cook (*Form Photograph* was the beginning of a long association of Chambers with this fine and still badly underrated poet), and Derek Mahon, whose *Ecclesiastes* provided the information that "The first 60 copies of this limited edition of 700 copies are signed by the author, numbered, bound in hard covers and priced at £1.05." New money, old offer. But even 700 may have seemed too many. For the 3rd series, which appeared in 1971, (Peter Scupham, Tony Curtis and Eddie Wainwright were among the six chosen poets), readers were told that "Sixty numbered copies of this first edition, specially bound in hard covers, have been signed by the author. (Price £1.05)". No longer a figure for the print run. Nor, after the first series, does the name of Eric Morten appear as co-editor. Instead, the second and third series are, we learn from the editorial information, "Edited and published by Harry Chambers with financial assistance from the North West Arts Association". (The second series alone carries an acknowledgement of a grant from the Leonard Cohen Trust. In noting this minutiae I feel rather like one of Larkin's scholars-manqués "wrapped up in personnels like old plaids".)

FORM PHOTOGRAPH
poems
STANLEY COOK

"Here the experience of the teacher in the classroom is itself the subject of the poem. There are 30 brief portraits in verse of the children in a class—any class, perhaps every class that one is ever likely to meet. They are all there, all the schoolboy archetypes: coward, sportsman, reprobate, narcissist, mimic, bookworm, snob, dreamer, buffoon. The individual portraits are telling, realistic, critical and at the same time sympathetic, never sentimental—infinitely better than anything D. H. Lawrence ever wrote about a classroom, and for humour, generosity and lightness of touch, almost as good as Chaucer's *Prologue*. **No teacher should be without a copy."**
THE TEACHER

HARRY CHAMBERS/PETERLOO POETS

Poetry pamphlets have always been integral to the publication of poetry, although I'm not clear as to when 32 pages began to emerge as "standard". (In the 1840s, Robert Browning issued his *Bells and Pomegrantes* in a series of what he called "pamphlets", one of which, "Dramatic Romances and Lyrics", ran to over a hundred pages.) Oscar Mellors' Fantasy Press, of the 1950s, had specialised in pam-phlets of various lengths, (for example Donald Davie's *The Brides of Reason* weighed in at 42 pp), but in the 1960s pamphlets tended towards the anorexic: Jon Silkin's Northern House sequences were often no more than 15 pages of text, and the pamphlets issued by the Byron Press which I co-edited took 12 pages of text as the norm. Phoenix Pamphlets at 11 pages of text, as *A Lough Neagh Sequence* came out at, were, therefore, nothing unusual. But the idea of producing the pamphlets in batches of six was new, and the fact that the series ran to three such batches was also unusual. (Most of us published pamphlets in an altogether more haphazard manner.) By 1972, the Phoenix series had gained a cachet as enviable as it was deserved, and the individual publications were widely noticed, and for the most part praised. I don't recall anyone even muttering about their somewhat provisional, even flimsy appearance. Pamphlets were supposed to be somehow fugitive publications. It was part of their charm.

But for Harry Chambers such charm was proving insufficient. The pamphlets were failing to gain the review coverage in the national literary press that they surely deserved, and it occurred to him that he would stand a better chance of achieving such coverage with fully-fledged volumes. So, time for a change. He applied to the Arts Council for funding to support collections of individual poets as replacement for the magazine, and although monies from that quarter weren't immediately forthcoming, he managed to persuade Eric J.Morten, the Didsbury bookseller whose name had been attached to the first series of pamphlets, to publish four full volumes in a hardback Peterloo Poets series, "Edited by Harry Chambers". The four were: *Signs of Life* by Stanley Cook, *The Snowing Globe* by Peter Scupham, both published in 1972, and *The*

Love Horse by John Mole and *Elsewhere* by David Selzer, a year later. In each case, the publisher was given as E.J.Morten. To some extent, the gambit paid off. All four well-produced volumes received extremely favourable reviews in, among other places, *Encounter* and the *Times Literary Supplement*. Eric Morten, however, declined to back a second series of volumes. Nevertheless, Harry had now decided to shut down the Phoenix pamphlet series, and only one more issue of the magazine was to appear, in Spring, 1975. Soon afterwards, Harry accepted the offer of a £2,000 grant from the Arts Council, given to assist him in the publication of a Peterloo Poets series of full-length collections. The first two such collections, Elma Mitchell's *The Poor Man in the Flesh* and *The Horwich Hennets* by Edmond Leo Wright were published in 1976, from a publishing address at Heaton Mersey, a south Manchester suburb.

Then came what Larkin might have called an "audacious, purifying,/Elemental move", from the North West to the South West of England. When Peterloo Poets produced its list of publications for 1976-78, the catalogue was issued from Treovis Farm Cottage, Upton Cross, Liskeard, Cornwall. The Chambers ménage, publisher, wife, daughter Hannah aged 5 and a growing book stock, had moved from outer Manchester, and the security of an income derived from a college lectureship, to the freedom and insecurity guaranteed by independent small-press publishing. A family holiday in which they had fallen for the attractions of Cornwall, combined with an offer from the college that provided a certain amount of money as well as early retirement, did the trick. And though money was never in great supply, and for years to come Harry would need to take on extra work – including stints as a marker of A-level English – it was now that Peterloo Poets began to establish itself as a press of the utmost distinction. A glance at the catalogue is enough to show how much the first two years achieved and why the *Times Literary Supplement* spoke for all when it commented that "Harry Chambers' Peterloo Poets series, an offshoot of his editing of *Phoenix*, shows the same flair and persistence that marks the magazine". There is, for example, *The Old Couple: Poems New & Selected* by F Pratt Green. Pratt Green was a Methodist minister whose earlier collection, *The Skating Parson*, had appeared from the Epworth Press. A good, entirely unfashionable poet, his work had made little impression until Peterloo brought out the Selected Poems. *The Old Couple* earned warm words from Blake Morrison, writing in the *Times Literary Supplement* while Fleur Adcock, reviewing the book for the P.E.N Newsletter, called it an "impressive collection". Such praise is entirely justified, although it is, we may think, less remarkable than the fact that they should notice the book at all. And for this, the reputation already won by Harry Chambers is all-important. Pratt Green's merits aren't in question, but it took the Peterloo imprint to bring him the attention he deserved. As for Stanley Cook, whose *Form Photograph* had been not only a lauded Phoenix pamphlet but one that, as I can testify from my own experience, quickly acquired a "secret" reputation, its re-publication in what was described as "improved format", to coincide with a new thirty poem sequence, *Staff Photograph*, together with another Cook pamphlet, *Alphabet*, which the author himself described as "concrete poetry", made 1976 something of an annus mirabilis for its author. It also showed how far in improving production values Peterloo Poets had come from the first series of Phoenix Pamphlets. To repeat, the pamphlets that made up that series had a decidedly provisional appearance. (Private press work – Mandeville, Dodman, Keepsake, etc. - was different because it was associated with those who – usually themselves writers – owned their own letterpress machines, most often an Albion, and who paid careful attention to typeface, font size, and paper, which might be bought direct from a paper mill. Those who ran such presses were and are the oenophiles of the small press world.)

But Peterloo Poets was clearly a break with the past, and not only because of the new colophon, a cartoon of a naked man – a holiday-maker? – up to his chest in water, his left hand holding a parasol above his head, absorbed in reading a book, presumably a volume of poetry, which he holds open with his right hand. Harry described to me the provenance of this logo. It was, he said, "a serendipitous find in a central Manchester second-hand bookshop". He had picked up for the proverbial song a 24 page pamphlet called *The Book Fool* described as a *Bibliophily in Caricature Supplement* to the American Book Collector (Metuchen, N.J. 1934). This consisted of a series of caricatures which first appeared in the famous German magazine for Book Lovers *Zeitschrift fur Bucherfreunde*, which began life soon after 1500 A.D. and came to an end in the middle years of the 19th century. The caricatures were made in woodcuts, copper engravings, original drawings, lithographs, aquatints, and etchings, and were of English, French and German origin.

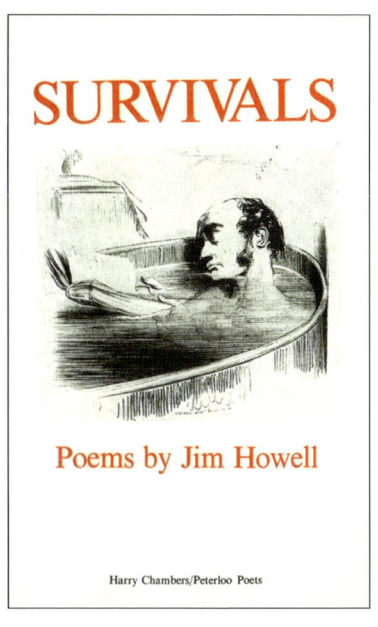

The logo Harry chose for Peterloo's colophon was a woodcut after Bertall from Briffanet's *Paris dans l'eau* (1844). All the caricatures depicted "love, folly, use and abuse of books in a grotesque manner", and Harry used further images from the same source for the cover illustration to Jim Howell's *Survivals* (Peterloo Poets, 1976) and for the Peterloo Previews 1 and 2 (1988 and 1989). By then he had established the annual series of magazines *Poetry Matters*, which Harry from the first identified as "quite simply and unashamedly a house journal for Peterloo Poets". To this end it provided a showcase for forthcoming Peterloo collections as well as, to quote from Harry's editorial to the first of such magazines (1983), publishing "forms of imaginative literature that are engaged in by poets on the Peterloo list". And, he added, "it will also publish reviews and criticism, not neglecting poetry of the past, and [it] will look outwards to the real world and the best of all other imaginative worlds". Poetry indeed matters and the slim annual, with its characteristic silver covers, on which the title was each year superimposed in different colour ink, became an essential part of the poetry scene. If you were an Associate Member – another wheeze for securing not merely money but loyalty – you got *Poetry Matters* for free. Others had to buy, but given the goodies within there was every reason to do so. Highlights included an article in No. 2 by U.A. Fanthorpe on her "Monet Project", the obituary of Philip Larkin by Harry in No. 4, which also featured among the Peterloo prize-winning poems about paintings that year (first prize to Carol Ann Duffy for "Virgin Punishing The Infant"), Keith Bosley's "Old Testament Emblems", with handsomely reproduced Holbein woodcuts. The following year's publication included a Wordsworth Symposium, with Beerbohm's famous cartoon of Wordsworth at odds in the Lake District, plus an autobiographical piece by U.A.Fanthorpe, "Slow Learner", an essential piece for any student of her work. Equally important, perhaps, is the feature in No. 8 on "New American Poetry", the notable Rimbaud Centenary celebration in No. 9, and then, in No. 10, centenarian features on both Whitman and Tennyson.

Back to the 70s. In addition to the press's new logo, the attractively-shaped pamphlets, slim-formatted after the manner of pocket books, had gloss-laminate card covers, the saddle-stitching was now secure, and the 12 point Garamond in which the texts were printed served them well. In addition, each of the actual twenty-six letters of *Alphabet*, as befits a pamphlet of concrete poems, is reproduced on page recto, facing the short poem to which it relates, and as no artist is credited with the visual work – bold black-and-white designs that look as though they were done with brush and ink – I assume they are Cook's own. And there is another matter to note. *Alphabet* is in toto 64 pps. As a result, it is spined, and although there is no lettering on the spine, the fact that

CENTENARY FEATURE
ARTHUR RIMBAUD
1854–1891

the book is perfect bound rather than saddle-stitched points to the future. Because from now on Peterloo Poets will be associated with full-length collections. Indeed, in the same year as *Staff Photograph* and *Alphabet*, Peterloo became publisher of a collection that won not only admirers, including such luminaries as Roy Fuller and Peter Porter, but which inevitably drew attention to the press's doings. The author, Edmond Leo Wright, himself described *The Horwich Hennets* as 46 poems selected "from a total of over 500. A hennet is a 12-line hendecasyllabic verse rhyming abacbcdedeff of which the first two feet are usually anapaestic." In fact, the third line of the very first poem has 13 syllables, and in later poems there are departures from the 11-syllable rule, but this doesn't greatly matter. (Marianne Moore, the great exemplar of syllabic verse, was by no means ready at all times to stick to her chosen syllabic count.) Writing in *Encounter*, Douglas Dunn had spoken for many when he remarked of *Staff Photograph* that "it calls the British publishing system in question that Stanley Cook failed to find a commercial publisher". Much the same might be said of the author of *The Horwich Hennets*, but with this proviso: that in its way, Peterloo Poets was, in some measure at least, a commercial publisher, and that Harry Chambers could now rightly consider himself, if not part of the "publishing system", then a publisher to whose door good poets would be beating a path.

That door was to remain near Liskeard for several years before the move to Calstock. By then Peterloo Poets had become almost *primus inter pares* of the leading group of small independent publishers. To say this is to state the obvious, but two matters need to be emphasised. The first is the very high rate of *succès d'estime* of Peterloo publications, the credit for which must go to Harry Chambers himself. He chose which poets to accept, he then edited their collections, and he saw to it that they appeared in a form that became as distinctive as it was unfailingly attractive: off-white, textured paper with well-designed and, customarily, four-colour covers. The second point to emphasise is that Peterloo Poets has probably done more than most publishers to promote women poets. Add this to the publisher's willingness to take a chance on poets who certainly can't be found along that reach of slack water where the more obtuse critics and commentators claim Peterloo poets lurk, and you have a far more adventurous press than Harry Chambers is sometimes given credit for running. Having said which, it is good to be able to note Herbert Lomas's praise for Donald Atkinson's *A Sleep of Drowned Fathers*, published by Peterloo in 1989, and of which Lomas, writing in *Ambit*, remarked, "this is an astonishing document to come out in England: Dosteyevskian in dolour, masochism, sadism, damnation and redemption. It is astounding, and also a triumph, that such material has found publication in this squeamish country – ready enough for violent entertainment but not enquiry into violence, and prone to covert censorship through petty office-holders and ad hoc publishing-house appointments." No such covert censorship for Peterloo.

Without doubt, the first important publication in this context was Elma Mitchell's *The Poor Man in the Flesh*. Like *The Horwich Hennets*, this appeared in 1976, and also like that publication it came to the notice of any number of discerning critics. Anne Stevenson, for instance, writing in *The Listener*, called it "surely one of the most compassionate, down-to-earth, feminine – not feminist – collections to appear in the last year", in *The Observer* Peter Porter remarked that Mitchell's "combination of keen observation and a talent for the proverbial gives great pleasure through out the book", and *The Sunday Times* reviewer, Julian Symons, expansively warm towards Mitchell's work, complained "That a poet so obviously and generously talented should not have been encouraged by a major publisher is regrettable". Well, yes, but why not praise the perspicacity of the publisher who had seen Mitchell's virtues and who later in *People Etcetera* (1987) put into print the following?

This Poem...

This poem is dangerous: it should not be left
Within the reach of children, or even of adults
Who might swallow it whole, with possibly
Undesirable side-effects. If you come across
An unattended, unidentified poem
In a public place, do not attempt to tackle it
Yourself. Send it (preferably in a sealed container)
To the nearest centre of learning, where it will be rendered
Harmless, by experts. Even the simplest poem
May destroy your immunity to human emotions.
All poems must carry a Government warning. Words
Can seriously affect your heart.

Appropriately enough, a fine coloured illustrated poster of this poem can be found in the Old Chapel at Calstock, which nowadays serves as Peterloo's headquarters.

It might seem invidious to pick out for special mention any one or two of the many good women poets that Peterloo Poets has encouraged over the years, but I can't resist mentioning the work of Joan Downar, M.R.Peacocke, Valerie Laws, Ann Drysdale and Rosamund Stanhope. Downar's two Peterloo collections, *The Empire of Light*, 1984, and *The Old Noise of Truth*, 1989, are alike remarkable for a lyricism that is capable of exploring human hurt and, just as tellingly, the erotic. So that when in "Parallel Worlds", from the first collection, she notes that "somewhere are people who harden/themselves to hunger, learn bird-like not to question,/or ask, and forbear to scream" we are aware that there is more of aghast wonder in this voice than any self-satisfied claim for her own sensitivity, and that love is at best a momentary counterweight against a world in which suffering is a daily norm. Yet love, too, makes its demands. Hence, a series of remarkable poems about a visit to Hindu temples to be found in *The Old Noise of Truth*, where the onlooker's attention is ineluctably drawn to "bodies, tenderly carved, tenderly curved/to each other their brown flesh cushioned/ and sweet, engorged with pleasure."

M.R.Peacocke is a poet for whose work I have an especial affection. It combines shrewd observation with a kind of un-illusioned tenderness of regard that is often turned in surprising directions. Of all her Peterloo collections it is *Selves* I most cherish, perhaps because until I came across it while reviewing for *Stand* I was insufficiently aware of her work. This is to take nothing away from her other collections, but it is to say that *Selves* was a revelation, one of those books that make you realise anew that there can never be any substitution for the true voice of poetry, the ways – by means of vowel, plosive, sibilant – it strikes inner ear. As in "Being Weasel": "To be weasel: to stain grasses/with jets of musk; to thieve/... to dance in bristling ellipses/intent upon a vein." What I reported in my 1996 review of this, I feel even more strongly now: "Just speaking those lines is pure pleasure."

Among the press's younger women poets, Valerie Laws is notable for the fact that she attracted Arts Council funding for a project to spray-paint poetry on sheep. She is also a poet a mere glance at whose work is enough to tell you that you are dealing with an imagination that doesn't so much go off the rails as see no need for them. Her first collection, *Moonbathing* has a number of poems whose titles are so throatgrabbing that you feel the poems themselves won't be able to live up to them: "Life's Too Short to Stuff a Mushroom", for example, or "Bones from a Medic's Dustbin", or "Showing Herr Hitler my New Shoes". Mostly, though, they can. And her second collection, *Quantum Sheep*, not only has its fair share of outré titles, it is stylistically and formally even more daring. It is also very funny: men everywhere can afford to laugh at "In Praise of Small Penises"("Come on, show us what you haven't got,/Let's see the last budgie in the shop").

The astonishingly prolific Ann Drysdale is a kindred spirit. Since 1995, when her debut volume for Peterloo *The Turn of the Cucumber* made its appearance, Harry Chambers has also published *Gay Science* (1999), *Backwork* (2002) and, in 2005, *Between Dryden and Duffy: Another Collection.* A highly-regarded poet and a prize-winner ("New Fruit" won second prize in the 2001 National Poetry Competition), Drysdale loves nothing better than to come at familiar subjects from an unfamiliar angle, usually comic or challenging, or to bounce in *faux-naif* fashion on well-upholstered solemnities. As funny about sex as Laws – "And if it rains, a closed car at four" begins "If the sun shines, we'll do it on the heath/ Behind the bandstand on the flattened grass./I'll wear the mink with nothing underneath" – she can also write with an exhilarating zest of moments when, as she says of the hare in "Running Through Dandelions", the sonnet with which she chooses to begin her most recent collection: "Rehearsing joy, anticipating fear,/He dances for the turning of the year." And as her skills at verse carpentry are seemingly inexhaustible, the pleasures of reading her are as varied as they are considerable. By comparison with such abundance, the late Rosamund Stanhope's output seems parsimonious in the extreme. But as width is no guarantee of quality, so the narrow seam may well be deep, and this is undoubtedly the case with Stanhope. Her two collections, *Lapidary* (1990) and *No Place for the Maudlin Heart*; (2001) are of great distinction. She had published poetry before Peterloo took her up, and her work was admired among those who knew of it, but it seems fair to say that the two Peterloo books did much to enhance the esteem in which she was held. "Please", from *Lapidary*, gives some idea of her power, her verbal attack, and her hard moral sense:

>today it is customary to
>request rather than command: 'Be so kind as
>not to point that thing at me'
>questions become complex:
>'where did you stash the
>grass?'
>statement is functional:
>'Mike lays Josie'

The Rev Robert Walker Skating on Doddingston Loch *by Sir Henry Raeburn is*

Poems by Brian Waltham
PETERLOO POETS

the later collection, is vivid with [...]nt: with the "bright/impressive [...]sh beyond the black resistors/and [...]"

[...]t is, it should be said, equally [...]s. And I suspect that some who [...]osen Peterloo simply because it's [...] they're more than happy to be [...]hn Mole, who began his writing [...] and then moved to Secker & [...] become a Peterloo poet, and his [...]ty that serves a poem's meaning [...]r than imposing on it, and wit hourly be while it can take on dark undertones, also lights up a relish for life's various dailinesses – make him in all senses an exemplary addition to the Peterloo list, as his recent, generous *Selected* shows. That he is also the author of a number of memorable poems about jazz musicians will no doubt have further endeared his publisher to him.

Mole began early. Not so Brian Waltham, who turned to poetry late in life and whose three Peterloo collections, *Music for Brass* (1990), *Masterclass* (1994) and *The Soldier on the Pier* (2002) were all published after his retirement from a career in the legal profession. Waltham's professional work makes comparatively little showing in his poetry, which does, however, reveal in ample worth his devotion to music. So, too, his delight in acute observation of landscape, although a sardonic edge keeps at bay the linking dangers of dewy-eyed sentimentality and mawkishness that frequently invade this territory. And Waltham's characteristic note of wry acceptance, his knowing-it-must-be-so, makes for poems which scrupulously balance outer and inner weathers.

> You can walk past the girl
> Made for you, hoping there
> Is someone made for her
> And then go back to what you
> Were thinking, if you can
> Remember what you were thinking.

The poem from which this comes, "Late Afternoon", the opening poem of Waltham's final collection, may at first look to be a scaled-down version of some Yeatsian lament for old age, but in fact its modest, anti-heroic stoicism gleams with moral sense: "It's helpful to look closely/At the sand./There are all sorts of/Small good things in sand." That very movingly exploits the cliché about the sands of time in order to provide a steadying assertion of what it is to be truly sentient.

John Whitworth would probably nod in agreement with the conclusion of "Late Afternoon", though I can also imagine him offering a rasping comment on any attempt to soften the blows that life stores up for us. There's a Juvenalian element to his way of thinking and seeing, and this is as patent in *Landscape with Small Humans*, a collection which Adam Thorpe in the *Observer* characterised as "a kind of *Songs of Innocence and Experience* filtered through a Fifties world of Fairy Soap and Ex-Lax, Ike and the King's death", as it is in "All You Need (to Know about Swinging London", from *The Whitworth Gun*.

> Late in 1967 Allen Ginsberg jets to London,
> Finds in Whistler's house on Cheyne Walk the party of the year,
> Twiggy girls in lace and velvet, dandy boys with tumbling ringlets,
> Neck and wrists are frothing ruffles – this is Aubrey Beardsley gear.
> Tapestries of unicorns are trembling on Augustan panels,
> Fitful shadows flit beneath the huge Moroccan chandelier.

In a quadraphonic whisper somewhere Sergeant Pepper plays.
Silent flunkies proffer brownies laced with hash on silver trays.
Let it all hang out and Let it be and Let it bleed.
All you need is Love. Love is all you need.

A certain Whitworthian affability invariably moderates savage indignation. That, and the sheer pleasure in making poems which, however they celebrate the disreputable and unmentionable (Whitworth wholeheartedly admires the work of the late Gavin Ewart) is always attentive to the craft of making. It's therefore not surprising that he should be a skilled parodist. Hence, *From the Sonnet History of Modern Poetry*, which both mocks and pays homage to those who are put in the firing line, including, for example, "Big Phil and Uncle John", "Crumpled lugubriousness in plain man's chat,/Moaning and muttering fuck from time to time,/The essential Englishness of being odd," and many others, all the way from Auden to Armitage.

David Sutton is different again. Commentators on his work have regularly cited as forbears such poets as Hardy, Edward Thomas and Larkin, which is accurate enough, though it risks making Sutton seem merely derivative. "Urban Grass" from his 1991 collection, *Settlements*, certainly begins on familiar ground: "Last of the green companions, grass,/You stand at bay in nature's pass/With banners threadbare but unfurled/Against a steel and concrete world." But what could be yet another piece of "genteel bellyaching" ends "I dreamed earth had its honour too/That lived, for all that we could do./I walked saluting in the street/The armies that will not retreat." Take the measure of "dreamed" and it's evident that this isn't a piece of windy optimism. Yet its affirmation is of a piece with the ending of John Clare's great poem, "The Flitting", which imagines grass springing "Where castles stood and grandeur died." What might at a glance seem sentimental is, in other words, given firmness of purpose by Sutton's discretion, his refusal to be drawn into unguarded utterance, and this, it hardly needs saying, characteristically makes for a scrupulous balancing which is as much moral as it is linguistic.

Sutton is in this respect – and in others, too – a poet who has a good deal in common with Maurice Rutherford, for whose two Peterloo collections, *This Day Dawning* (1989) and *Love is a Four-Letter World* (1994) I have an especial regard. The former is remarkable for the section "Snapshots in a Shipyard", although "snapshots" hardly does justice to the deeply-considered and exactly-crafted observations that run through these poems, for example, the "Old Book-Keeper", whose life is "a double-entry system: work/a force-fed virtue, all daydreams debited", or the "Fitter", who, a rambler when he's free from work, "knows widgeon and the flight of lapwings,/hears the blackbird writing the score for dawn/above the plainsong of the wind". The language of occupation here defines men, their shaped and in some ways thwarted lives, in a manner and with a degree of imaginative sympathy Dickens would have understood and approved, because it also becomes a way of reclaiming their individuality. It is in no sense reductive. And this imaginative generosity is even more powerfully at work in *Love is a Four-Letter World*, as in "September Outings", a poem which, while it pays fitting tribute to Larkin, the poet by whom the Hull-born Rutherford is most affected, is also by way of being a magisterial revisiting and in some ways criticism of "Whitsun Weddings". Hence, the final stanza:

> In brass-lined boardrooms up and down the land
>   deep in regret
> a million more redundancies get planned,
> while chairmen's hiked-up salaries are set,
> and Urban Councils chase arrears in rents,
> wideboys, insiderdealers, some M.Ps
> grow richer by a second home in Spain,
> a custom-plated white Mercedes-Benz,
> that new portfolio. True-blue disease.
> the spores of loss, somewhere becoming gain.

Equally relishing the chance to make poems out of being non-metropolitan, William Scammell moves more readily than Rutherford to satire. His is the quizzical, sceptical eye glimpsed among the protective or plainly reverential gaze of onlookers at the social scene, especially perhaps in his 1985 collection, *Jouissance*, where an alert attention to human waywardness is off-set by a more speculative tone, even hesitancy, as though Scammell is consciously guarding against, even rebuking himself for, the unholy delight with which he can run to judgement. But what is never absent from his work is the evident pleasure in the act of writing itself, in the display of formal virtuosity and linguistic reach. And so "Whiteout" opens

> After the meal and the jazz and the conversation
> which required a Cumbrian Saturday winter evening
> the front door opened on an unbid tempest
> of intemperate wind and snow, chthonic chaos
> storming about the lamps, a whole demented sky
> in self-analysis, singing as it bounced on by
> past Skiddaw, Great Hall and Loughrigg Ring
> as though it meant to warn and waken everything
> with its sublime erratum...

The unremarkable, almost humdrum note of the opening is displaced by the sudden energy of the storm which erupts into the poem as though it was bidden by Scammell's imagination alone, in need of some further stimulus to fire it up, the phrases no sooner set down than they are displaced by others in this helter-skelter of word and image making.

A much younger poet, Steven Blyth, has something of Scammell's energy, although his gaze perhaps moves more slowly over "the interiors of a quotidian Britain", to use a phrase coined by Stephen Knight in his review for the *Times Literary Supplement* of Blyth's collection, *Baddy*. This allows for a measured look at, if not the worst that Hardy recommended, at all events the seamy underside of life. And so, of death, he comments: "The makers of fiction/Have got it wrong. Usually bowels are opened,/There's vomit, loads of blood." Well, no, not necessarily, but Blyth's refusal to be seduced by comfort, whether of word or deed, makes his collection a bracing alternative to conventional pieties, and his choice of subject – as, for example, the understudy who knows the lines but lets his fellow actors flounder when they dry – characteristically directs attention to the odd, the misfits, the disquieting nay-sayers. This is a point worth making, not merely because the work of poets such as Whitworth, Scammell and Blyth convincingly rebuts the still-lingering myth of Peterloo as a home for those whose axe needs no grinding but only because it is all handle and no head, but also because it shows how alert Harry Chambers remains to writers who don't fit into any expected role. Their publisher requires merely that they should write well and have something interesting to say. But it is quite wrong to put about any such statement as that Peterloo plays host only to those who are "traditionalists", if by that is meant that it is a home for the passé. It was that no-nonsense modernist, poet and acerbic critic, Edgell Rickword who long ago laid down a dictum to which I can imagine Chambers giving his whole-hearted assent: "theories about the way to write poetry are utterly useless. It is obvious that poetry may be written in a hundred ways, in the rhythms of normal speech, of prose, of a merry-go-round, or even in cadence." Amen to that.

Anyone scanning the Peterloo list is in fact far less likely to come away muttering of sameness than to be struck by its variety. And that Chambers remains hospitable to the work of interesting younger writers can be verified by a quick glance at more recent publications, among them collections by Wayne Burrows, Tim Cunningham, Owen Gallagher and Alyson Hallett. Burrows *Marginalia* (2001) is an ambitious, intriguing collection much influenced by surrealism and the less earth-tethered of 17th Century poets, so that even the most ordinary of sights is given a kind of vertiginous glamour: "Trees unravel at the edge of the field/like estuaries, arteries,/tentacles lifting the moon to its hook,/clear of the borealis/ headlamps make." Tim Cunningham, an older man, is to date the author of two collections, *Don Marcelino's Daughter* (2001) and *Unequal Thirds* (2006). Cunningham has a strong imagination much exercised by the bizarre and sometimes cruel incongruities of time, of history, of place, as in the very fine "Female Nude, circa 1916", which begins in the silence which is "the anthem/Fit for no-man's-land, for foetal/Bodies draped/Like weekend washing across lines/Of viper wire". Reading this you think you are to be faced with yet another poem about the horrors of the Great War. And so you are, but with a difference: for at about the time an attack is to start and as count-down

> Ticks towards the whistles
> For over-the-top commands...
> ... a police commissioner
> On the Rue Taitbout is
> Tearing down Modigliani nudes,
> Affronted by full frontal pubic hair.

This isn't making a cheaply ironic point. If there is an irony it is on a huge scale: of the conventional proprieties of a death-dealing world keeping the appointed time of its rendezvous with mass murder, set against, and triumphing over, the essential life-affirming nature of what is "improper".

Incongruity also features in Owen Gallagher's *Sat Guru Snowman*, yet another Peterloo publication of 2001. Indeed, incongruity could almost said to be its defining mode: one that allows the poet to engage with matter ranging from the comic to an altogether more grievous, dangerous engagement with the oddities of personal and social history. The opening, title, poem wittily and rather beautifully celebrates a kind of urban myth of multiculturalism, in which small boys "Satnam and Sarwan built a snowman" as a result of which

Sat Guru Snowman

*Poems by
Owen Gallagher*

PETERLOO POETS

> Next day
> the school playground was full of Sikh snowmen.
>
> Some wore top-knots that looked like mushrooms.
> Unused Diwali candles lit them at night.

Elsewhere though, the tone is darker, its hesitancy serving to take the measure of life's happenstance, as in "Post-Mortem", where the poet records his mother telling him of his father's fatal heart attack, which happened while he was "laying pipes like arteries/into the heart of the hospital", and of how, "the foreman ordering him home/without pay" (the line-break is perfectly judged) he stopped off

> at the Off-Licence
> for a miniature of brandy.
> How she found him curled up
> on the bedroom floor,
> the seal of the bottle
> unbroken on their anniversary.

This necessarily risks sentimentality in order to achieve what is surely an authentic ending, in which tenderness outflanks wonderment.

Alyson Hallett's *The Stone Library* (2007) is marked by its engagements, often baffled or thwarted but persistent, with the outer world, most intriguingly developed perhaps in "Sunday", where the speaker by the sea learns a Jacottet poem,

> clumsily reciting to an audience
> of rocks and seals
>
> 'Je ne voudrais qu'éloigner
> ce qui nous sépare du claire'

> I only want to remove
> that which separates us from the light,

and then reflects that "Jacottet is the mother/of space./He unoccupied the page/with words." Elsewhere, she deals in the moment of surprise that triggers narrative, as in "Jealous of Jesus' Feet", which begins, "Tavistock: early afternoon, belly full of sea bass/and chilled South African white. I'm looking/for a place to cry..." New readers, as they say, begin here. Or, if you prefer, begin at "Foothills Girl", which opens with the declaration that "I'm a dedicated foothills girl/dreaming where the stream runs fast/ and trees screech towards the sky". All these poets have been well served by a publisher whose loyal devotion to the cause of contemporary poetry is second to none. But I imagine that even he would accept that such loyalty has been amply repaid by the outstanding poet whom he first published nearly 30 years ago, and who since then has become one of the most widely and highly acclaimed of living poets.

U.A.Fanthorpe stands out as not only representing Peterloo's most obvious success, but as embodying its values. Her first collection, *Side Effects*, was published in 1978. I'm not sure how many years it was before, in Liz Lochhead's often quoted praise, the poet was recognised as "a national treasure", but my guess is that it didn't take long. As Sean O'Brien commented in *The Sunday Times* "good poets who are popular are hard to come by. Since her first book *Side Effects* appeared in 1978, U.A.Fanthorpe has moved effortlessly towards that status." True, I once wrote of a collection of William Scammell's which I was reviewing for *The New Statesman*, that "Scammell is the luck any small publisher deserves". I stand by that. But how much truer it is of Fanthorpe, and not only because of her excellence as a poet. It is, of course, the kind of poetic excellence that Peterloo celebrates and endlessly encourages: formally adroit, capable of moving between opposite poles of the sombre and comic without loss of poise, addressing concerns that are knowable and therefore shareable but without simplification (or condescension), using the resources of metaphor and, more daringly, of commonplace language in such a way as to prise open their deeper implications. It's heartening that so exemplary a poet should have been awarded the Queen's Gold Medal for Poetry (in 2003), still more heartening that poems of hers should be on A Level syllabuses, most heartening of all that her books sell out and that her *Collected Poems 1978-2003* should have appeared from Peterloo (2005) in a splendid hard-back edition, as well as in paper-back. (Though in a brief Foreword she permits herself to lament that this means losing "the beautiful inventive covers that Harry Chambers and his wife Lynn picked for each individual book".) There is no doubt that merely for being U.A.Fanthorpe's publisher, Harry Chambers deserves our lasting gratitude. Equally, he must be grateful that her collections bring Peterloo such financial rewards.

Ah, finance. From the start, Peterloo Poets has been supported by grants from the Arts Council, first of Great Britain, latterly England. And there have been other benefactors, notably the National Lottery. This isn't the place to provide a blow by blow account of how the Press has coped with financial matters in a world where there is always uncertainty, but it would be wrong not to mention at least some of the ways in which the Chambers blend of ingenuity and resolve have combined with a wide understanding of poetry in order to prevent Peterloo from settling into complacency and therefore becoming at all vulnerable to the charge that as it's doing nothing new it therefore doesn't deserve official – for which read Arts Council – support. Hence, to take one example among many that could be cited, the press's already mentioned annual Open Poetry Competition, which began in 1985, and whose early sponsors include *The Independent*, *The Guardian* and *Marks and Spencer*, has long been a major presence in UK poetry, each year attracting thousands of entries which are judged by panels of distinguished poets.

"The annual Peterloo competition is one of the major events of the poetry calendar. There are a great many people in this country writing poetry and the opportunities for recognition are few. A competition offers the possibility that your poem will rise to the top of the pile, since it presents itself anonymously, and is judged on merit alone. It is not uncommon for the first prize-winner in a competition to be someone who has never published a poem before, as was the case in 2006 with 1st prize winner Laura Thompson and 4th prize winner Victoria Cichy."

Carole Satyamurti, Judges' Report, Peterloo 2007 Competition

Natural Selection

1st Prize, 2006

Like suns they lord it over the chaos,
The great glass orbs that light the classrooms,
The ragged-trousered rowdies splashing water,
And the tiny timid ones who cry for home.

In the next form up they have progressed
To black sugar-paper, which they cover
With yellow stars and moons, a blue strip
For the firmament, skirted blobs for mother.

Then, reading: ribboning out from mysterious
Hidden spinnerets, acrobats, they take flight,
Baby spiders, on the first miraculous thread
Across the tree of words: lustrous, infinite.

Then they are naming things: *cygnet* and *sycamore*,
Growing alum crystals and acorns,

Watching slithering spawn dissolve into
A shriggle of tadpoles, a font of semicolons,

As if to say what's next? *I* am next,
Glowers Mrs Mitchell, now you are the big ones.
To you I will say divide and multiply,
For there are hard times ahead, harder even than sums.

She wipes the coloured chalk animals
From the blackboard with a swoosh, a splat.
This is our world, this milky whirl of dust,
Where we make ourselves. Now think on *that*.

Laura Thompson

Missing

4th Prize, 2006

At her bedside, a box of milk teeth;
a crayoned card, clumsy with love.
His face in the mirror, the doorway, still there
with impossible clues: three years, seven weeks.
The days rise to meet her like bile in her throat;
she scans passing faces through net curtain shrouds.
In the hallway she runs to each knell of the phone
as the rust on his bicycle flakes like dried blood.
Every night she wakes, hearing him scream:
her prayers rise as moths to the moon.

Her prayers rise as moths to the moon
every night. She wakes hearing him scream
as the rust on his bicycle flakes like dried blood
in the hallway. She runs to each knell of the phone;

she scans passing faces. Through net curtain shrouds
the days rise to meet her, like bile in her throat,
with impossible clues – three years, seven weeks.
His face in the mirror, the doorway. Still there.
A crayoned card, clumsy with love,
at her bedside. A box of milk teeth.

Victoria Cichy

The Competition is guaranteed to make money, and as it happened money also came from selling to Puffin two outstandingly good books of children's poetry by John Mole, both of which originally appeared under the Peterloo imprint: *Boo to a Goose* (1987), which won the prestigious Signal (Poetry for Children) Award for 1988, and *The Mad Parrot's Countdown* 1990). In addition, selling to King Penguin the paperback rights of U.A.Fanthorpe's *Selected Poems* in 1986 can't have put a dent in Peterloo's bank balance. But there was no certainty of financial gain in undertaking to publish collections of poetry by a number of non UK poets. Far from it.

On the other hand, a less material form of enrichment has undoubtedly come from Peterloo's bringing out books from the internationally-admired American poet, Dana Gioia, from the outstanding Caribbean poet Ian MacDonald and the Canadians Brian Bartlett and Gary Geddes, and from its taking on work by the Irish poet Gabriel Fitzmaurice and the Irish-domiciled Mark Roper. I imagine that Harry Chambers will have felt both gratified and vindicated when Roper's *The Hen Ark* was the winner of the 1992 Aldeburgh Poetry Festival Award for the year's best first collection of poetry, the third winner in succession for Peterloo Poets. (Donald Atkinson's *A Sleep of Drowned Fathers* was adjudged winner in 1991, and the year before that my own *Studying Grosz on the Bus* took the prize.)

MERCY WARD

Poems by Ian McDonald

PETERLOO POETS

"Ian McDonald's *Mercy Ward* is a superb collection, a series of stories, character portraits and lyrics derived from McDonald's experience as a hospital visitor in Guyana. The ward is where the old and poor come to die, be it slowly or soon, and McDonald's recreation of the life of the place is by turns hilarious and moving as the loves and accomplishments, fears and furies of the inmates unfold. It would be very hard to find work from this country to compare in rhythmic attack or emotional directness."

Sean O'Brien, *Times Literary Supplement*

Peterloo also deserves the gratitude of anyone interested in poetry for publishing in 1995 Christopher Pilling's splendid translation of Corbière's *Les Amours Jaunes/ These Jaundiced Loves*, in a bilingual edition of 400 plus pages. The book, beautifully produced, was launched in Roscoff with a champagne reception hosted by the mayor, an occasion which will have brought the publisher a good deal of satisfaction, given his love for French poetry (he knows and can quote by heart poems by, among others, Baudelaire, Gérard de Nerval and Verlaine), and his shrewd appreciation of good wine.

A year later, the Press took the momentous decision to put in a bid for proper headquarters. Up until that point this most cherishable of publishing enterprises had always been run from home: look at the editorial page of any Peterloo collection until the late 90s and you can trace the publisher's movements: from Didsbury, to Stockport, to Treovis Farm Cottage, Liskeard, to Kelly Gardens, Calstock. By the time the caravanserai took on this last address, the press's back stock had inevitably grown to such an extent that housing it was a major problem. I remember looking along the shelving in what had, I assume, been a back bedroom at Kelly Gardens, and thinking that one touch of kindling would make the whole world of Peterloo flame. It was only commonsense to search for some affordable proper storage space. And, given that the press was a round-the-clock commitment, one to which Lynn Chambers, now salaried and acting as full-time Administrator and much else besides, gave as much time as her husband, there was also a need for proper office space. A couple of rooms above a shop, perhaps? A lock-up garage with add-on office? Well, no.

"In 1996 the Trustees of Peterloo Poets took the risk of buying the Old Chapel, Calstock, for £50,000, with the aid of a £15,000 loan from Nat West (long paid off) and a £35,000 grant from the Po Shing Woo foundation." These are the publisher's own words, a précis of events which continues by noting that with the aid of an Arts Council Lottery Capital Grant of £211, 665, it was possible to convert the Chapel to a suitable office and warehouse for Peterloo to operate from. Harry further notes that "Peterloo succeeded in raising £150,000 (approx) in matching funding before construction work could start, and moved into its new premises in late August 1999." What no-one who hasn't seen Peterloo's headquarters could guess from this dry summary is that the Old Chapel is a stunning piece of conversion. So stunning, in fact, that the work has won two awards for the company who undertook the work, Stephen Whettem, Architects, Tavistock. In 1999, it received a "Special Commendation" from the Cornish Buildings Group, and two years later was named by Caradon District Council for "Best Scheme in the Non-Residential Conversion/Restoration" category. From the outside, all is much as you'd expect from the building's nomenclature. Grey featureless stone, slate roof, arched neo-Gothic entrance. The kind of chapel building that could once be seen the length and breadth of England, home to dwindling congregations, until, windows smashed and roof fallen in, they were sold off to be used as car showrooms, carpet warehouses, or went under the developer's ball and chain. Even in their heyday it's easy to imagine these buildings as dark and cheerless. For all I know, The Old Chapel at Calstock may have been just such a place.

But step inside the converted building and you're in a world of light. For the rear south facing wall has been knocked out and replaced by glass. The effect is magical. You look not at enclosing stone-work but out and over the river Tamar to hilly fields where cows roam and, above and beyond, a wide sky stretches. It's impossible not to feel that this ought to be a place to which poets should hasten.

And so they do. Since its conversion the Old Chapel has opened its doors to numerous audiences for occasions connected with the performance and celebration of poetry. On a Sunday evening in July 2000 John Mole and I – he on clarinet, on cornet, me, played and read to a packed house, an occasion made memorable, for me at least, because the support musicians we'd been promised failed to appear. We had therefore no choice but to borrow the drummer and bass-guitarist from a rock group also on the bill, neither of whom had heard of four-four time. The resulting music may well have constituted the only example in history of free-form Chicago Jazz. To our astonishment, the audience seemed not to notice that anything was amiss, a matter I'm prepared tentatively to trace to the fact that not only did the wine flow, but that as Harry may have forgotten to apply for a music licence every window in the place remained shut for the whole of that sultry evening. What we took for applause could have been people stirring the increasingly heated air in hope of creating some faint breeze.

Rather more orthodox programmes at the Chapel, while including jazz, have featured a wide variety of poets from Fleur Adcock to Kit Wright, as well as international Poetry Festivals that have included Wendy Cope, U.A.Fanthorpe, Dana Gioia, Michael

Donaghy, Ann Drysdale, Gary Geddes, Jackie Kay, Michael Longley, Les Murray, Mario Petrucci, Peter Porter and Lawrence Sail. (The three-day festival held during the first weekend of September, 2006, was the eighth: among the poets reading their work were Jean 'Binta' Breeze, Peter and Anne Sansom and Kenneth Steven.) And by opening its doors to story-tellers, singers and musicians of different persuasions the Chapel has been a place of general cultural resource. A great and a good thing.

But the Old Chapel, Calstock, also proved to be, if not the chapel perilous, then a chapel under peril of closure, when in 2000 its continuous funding by the Arts Council was unexpectedly threatened. The threat came at a very bad moment. For months Harry Chambers had been helping to nurse his ailing wife and now, at more or less the same moment that she died, he was served the news that South West Arts proposed to cease funding Peterloo. It's a measure of the respect and affection that Harry enjoys, that there was an immediate, sustained and increasingly widespread outcry at this proposed act of cultural vandalism, one that no doubt surprised those who had thought up the scheme to deprive Peterloo of its money. They must have been as surprised by the publisher's cussed refusal to roll over and die. Instead, he fought back, and with help from his many friends, some but by no means all in high places, he ensured that the threat was withdrawn. Good. In fact, very good. And even better that a second crisis over the withdrawal of funding was successfully fought off in 2005.

Some may think "cussed" not the right word to use here. I don't know, though. From the age of fourteen, Harry Chambers has been adept at finding his way about a tennis court, and for some years he was good enough to play at county level. So was Bill Scammell. The pair were on the same side of the net when they met in London to research the photographs for *The Game: Tennis Poems*, which Bill edited and Peterloo published in 1992. Their ferreting for suitable pictures took them first to the Wimbledon Lawn Tennis Museum and then to the Hulton Picture Library, where, according to Harry, they unearthed "wonderful sepia photographs of Suzanne

Lenglen (used on both front and back covers of the subsequent book) and Big Bill Tilden, and classic photographs of John McEnroe, Arthur Ashe, Evonne Goolagong, Lew Hoad, Bjorn Borg, Hanna Mandlikova and other greats". The resulting book, very evidently a labour of love, became the *Independent*'s Sports Book of the Year, although sales were disappointing. In Harry's own words, *The Game* "alienated tennis lovers who didn't like poetry and poetry lovers who didn't like tennis". Whether poet and publisher ever faced each other on opposites sides of the net, I don't know, but I imagine Bill as the more terrier-like, scrapping, scurrying about the court, whereas Harry – whose preferred surface I fancy to have been clay – will have gone about accumulating points altogether more steadily, even implacably. He himself sets great store by some words spoken by a clockwork elephant to be found in one of his favourite novels, Russell Hoban's *The Mouse and His Child*: "... one simply goes out into the world and does whatever one does. One dances or balances a ball, as the case may be. One does what one is wound to do." But such doing implies both obduracy and staying power. These are qualities that come in handy for a publisher, especially one who finds himself having to fight against the ways of bureaucracy. Add to them those other virtues I have touched on and you have the very model of what's needed to sustain a small independent press for as long, as successfully, and as wholly admirably as Harry Chambers has sustained Peterloo Poets.

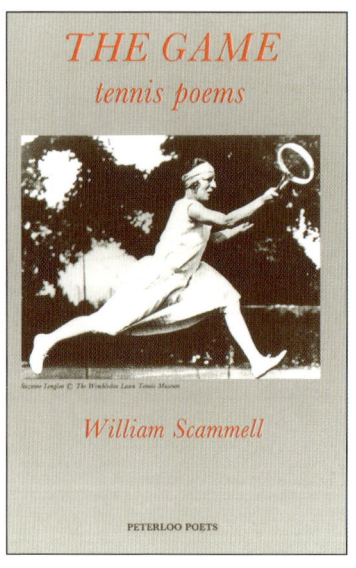

PETERLOO PREVIEW 1

Cover illustration: Woodcut after Bertall from Texier, *Tableaux de Paris* (1852–1853)

Donna Dickenson   Stephen Duncan
Tony Roberts   Raymond Tallis
Brian Waltham   Maureen Wilkinson

1988

Photograph by Steve Whettem

The Old Chapel, Calstock